SIMPLIFIED STRATEGIES FOR BUILDING WEALTH IN 2024 AND BEYOND

CHARTING YOUR PATH TO FINANCIAL FREEDOM AND ABUNDANT LIVING

By

ANDREW MARK

Table Of Contents

Andrew Mark

INTRODUCTION

In the ever-evolving landscape of finance and economics, the pursuit of wealth building stands as a cornerstone of personal and societal prosperity. As we venture into 2024, the importance of understanding wealth building has never been more critical. The global economic climate, shaped by technological advancements, geopolitical shifts, and societal transformations, presents both unprecedented opportunities and unforeseen challenges for individuals seeking financial security and abundance.

In this book, we embark on a journey to unravel the complexities of wealth building in the contemporary world. We delve into the strategies and principles that resonate in the dynamic environment of 2024, empowering readers to navigate the intricacies of wealth creation with confidence and clarity.

Central to our exploration is the recognition that simplicity is paramount. In an age inundated with information and options, simplified strategies serve as beacons of effectiveness amidst the noise. By distilling the essential components of wealth building, we equip readers with actionable insights and practical tools to forge their paths towards financial independence and abundance.

Join us as we uncover the timeless principles and innovative approaches that define wealth building in 2024. Together, let us embark on a journey towards financial empowerment and fulfillment in the rapidly evolving landscape of the 21st century.

CHAPTER ONE

SETTING THE FOUNDATION

In the hustle of daily life, it's easy to overlook our financial health until it demands our attention with urgency. Yet, taking a moment to assess our current financial situation is not just a practical necessity; it's a soul-searching journey that reveals our values, aspirations, and fears.

Begin this introspection by confronting your financial reality head-on. Gather your financial statements, bank statements, bills, and any other relevant documents. Take stock of your income, expenses, debts, and savings. This raw data forms the foundation of your financial self-awareness.

Next, delve deeper into the emotional landscape surrounding your finances. What are your financial goals and dreams? Do you aspire to buy a home, travel the world, or retire comfortably? Conversely, what are your financial anxieties? Are you worried about debt, job stability, or unexpected expenses? Acknowledging these aspirations and fears is crucial in understanding the driving forces behind your financial decisions.

Reflect on your spending habits and lifestyle choices. Are your expenses aligned with your values and goals? Are you living within your means, or are you stretching beyond, accumulating debt in the process? Recognize the difference between needs and wants, and evaluate whether your spending brings you lasting fulfillment or momentary gratification.

Consider your relationship with money. How do you view wealth, success, and material possessions? Are you driven by a scarcity mindset, constantly chasing more, or do you embrace abundance and gratitude for what you already have? Your beliefs about money profoundly influence your financial behaviors and outcomes.

Finally, assess your financial knowledge and skills. Are you equipped with the necessary tools to manage your finances effectively? If not, seek out resources, education, or professional guidance to improve your financial literacy and empower yourself to make informed decisions.

Assessing your current financial situation transcends mere number-crunching; it's an intimate exploration of your values, aspirations, and beliefs. Embrace this soul-searching journey with honesty and courage, for in understanding your financial self, you pave the path towards a future of security, abundance, and fulfillment.

DEFINING YOUR FINANCIAL GOALS FOR 2024

As we step into the new year, it's imperative to embark on a journey of introspection and practicality when it comes to defining our financial goals for 2024. Beyond mere numbers and budgets, this endeavor demands a deeper exploration of our values, aspirations, and the legacy we wish to create.

Firstly, let's embrace practicality. Begin by conducting a thorough review of your current financial situation. Take stock of your income, expenses, debts, and investments. Reflect on past spending habits and identify areas for improvement. Set clear, achievable objectives that align with your financial reality. Whether it's paying off debt, saving for a down payment, or investing for retirement, specificity is key. Break down larger goals into smaller, manageable milestones to track progress effectively throughout the year.

However, financial goal-setting isn't solely about numbers—it's also a soul-searching journey. Take the time to ponder your deepest desires and dreams. What truly matters to you beyond material wealth? Perhaps it's the freedom to pursue passions, the ability to support loved ones, or the opportunity to give back to your community. These intrinsic motivations will fuel your commitment to financial success and imbue your journey with purpose.

Furthermore, consider the legacy you wish to leave behind. How do you envision your financial decisions impacting future generations? Cultivate a mindset of abundance and generosity, striving not only to secure your own future but also to uplift others along the way. Whether through charitable giving, educational initiatives, or sustainable investments, let your financial goals reflect a commitment to leaving the world a better place than you found it.

In point of fact, defining your financial goals for 2024 is a dual journey of practicality and soul-searching. By marrying pragmatic planning with heartfelt introspection, you can chart a course towards financial empowerment and fulfillment. Remember, it's not just about the destination—it's about the journey and the person you become along the way. So, as you set sail into the sea of possibilities that this new year holds, may you navigate with wisdom, purpose, and an unwavering commitment to your financial well-being and beyond.

CHAPTER TWO

BUDGETING BASICS

In the labyrinth of financial planning, 2024 presents itself as a year of shifting paradigms and evolving priorities. Crafting a realistic budget amidst these dynamics demands more than number crunching; it requires soul-searching. Here's a pragmatic guide to sculpting a budget that not only aligns with your financial reality but also resonates with your deepest aspirations.

1. **Self-Reflection**: Begin by introspecting your values, goals, and aspirations. What do you truly want to achieve in 2024? Whether it's financial freedom, career advancement, or personal growth, understanding your motivations is crucial.

2. **Assessing Income**: Take stock of all income streams, including salary, freelance gigs, investments, and passive income. Be realistic about potential fluctuations and uncertainties, such as market volatility or job instability.

3. **Tracking Expenses**: Scrutinize your spending habits over the past few months. Categorize expenses into essentials (e.g., rent, groceries) and discretionary (e.g., dining out, entertainment). Identify areas where you can trim unnecessary expenditures without sacrificing joy or fulfillment.

4. **Setting Priorities**: Prioritize your financial goals based on their significance and urgency. Whether it's building an emergency fund, paying off debt, or saving for a milestone, allocate resources accordingly. Consider the 50/30/20 rule: 50% for essentials, 30% for

discretionary spending, and 20% for savings and debt repayment.

5. **Creating a Budget**: Use budgeting tools or apps to streamline the process. Set realistic limits for each spending category, ensuring that your budget reflects both your needs and desires. Embrace flexibility to accommodate unexpected expenses or opportunities.

Example:

Let's say your monthly income is $4,000. After deducting essentials ($2,000) and allocating for discretionary spending ($1,200), you're left with $800 for savings and debt repayment. If your goal is to save $5,000 by the end of the year, aim to save around $417 each month.

Crafting a realistic budget in 2024 is not merely about numbers; it's about aligning your financial decisions with your values and aspirations. By embarking on this journey of self-discovery and fiscal responsibility, you pave the path towards a more empowered and fulfilling future.

STRATEGIES FOR MANAGING EXPENSES

In a world marked by economic uncertainties and rapid technological advancements, crafting a realistic strategy becomes paramount.

Step 1: Self-Reflection

Begin by delving into your values and financial goals. What brings you fulfillment, and what are your long-term aspirations? This soul-searching process lays the foundation for an expense management plan aligned with your life's purpose.

Step 2: Categorize and Prioritize

Divide your expenses into categories, distinguishing between needs and wants. Prioritize essentials such as housing, utilities, and groceries over non-essential spending like entertainment and luxury items. Embrace minimalism as a guiding principle.

Step 3: Budgeting Tools

Leverage modern budgeting tools and apps to streamline the process. Platforms like Mint, YNAB, or PocketGuard provide real-time insights into your spending habits, helping you stay accountable to your financial goals.

Step 4: Emergency Fund

In 2024, unpredictable events can impact finances. Build a robust emergency fund equal to at least three to six months of living expenses. This safety net acts as a buffer during unexpected setbacks, fostering financial resilience.

Step 5: Sustainable Living

Embrace sustainable living practices to both reduce expenses and contribute to a healthier planet. Evaluate eco-friendly options for transportation, energy consumption, and daily choices. This not only aligns with a global ethos but often proves cost-effective in the long run.

Example: Sarah's Sustainable Budget

Sarah, inspired by eco-conscious living, opts for a bicycle commute, reducing transportation costs. She invests in energy-efficient appliances, cutting down utility bills. These choices align with her values and substantially contribute to her monthly savings.

In 2024, managing expenses transcends mere number-crunching; it's a reflection of personal values and a commitment to a sustainable future. By integrating practical budgeting techniques with a soul-searching mindset, individuals can navigate the financial landscape with resilience and purpose.

CHAPTER THREE

SAVING AND INVESTING

Saving and investing are crucial for several reasons:

1. Financial Security: Saving and investing help individuals build a financial cushion for emergencies and unexpected expenses. This financial security can provide peace of mind and reduce stress during challenging times.

2. Achieving Financial Goals: Whether it's buying a house, funding education, starting a business, or retiring comfortably, saving and investing are essential for reaching long-term financial goals. Regular saving and wise investing can help grow wealth over time.

3. Beating Inflation: Keeping money in savings without investing it might not keep up with inflation. Inflation reduces the purchasing power of money over time.

Investing allows your money to grow at a rate that typically outpaces inflation, preserving your purchasing power.

4. Retirement Planning: Saving and investing are crucial for retirement planning. With the decline of traditional pension plans, individuals must rely on their own savings and investments to fund their retirement. Starting to save and invest early can lead to significant growth over several decades.

5. Building Wealth: Investing allows individuals to grow their wealth over time. By investing in assets such as stocks, bonds, real estate, or mutual funds, individuals have the potential to earn returns that exceed what they would get from traditional savings accounts.

6. Financial Independence: Saving and investing can lead to financial independence, where individuals have enough wealth to cover their living expenses without needing to work actively for income. Achieving financial independence provides flexibility and freedom in how individuals choose to live their lives.

7. Passive Income Generation: Investing in income-generating assets such as dividend-paying stocks, rental properties, or bonds can provide a steady stream of passive income. This income can supplement earnings from work and contribute to financial stability.

8. Economic Growth: Saving and investing also play a crucial role in economic growth. When individuals and businesses save and invest, they contribute to capital formation, which fuels economic expansion, creates jobs, and drives innovation.

Overall, saving and investing are fundamental components of personal finance that can lead to financial stability, growth, and the achievement of long-term financial goals.

BUILDING AN EMERGENCY FUND

Establishing an emergency fund is not just prudent—it's essential. Whether it's unexpected medical expenses, car repairs, or sudden job loss, having a financial safety net can provide peace of mind and mitigate the impact of unforeseen events. Here, we'll outline practical steps to create a realistic emergency fund tailored to the unique challenges of 2024.

1. Assess Your Financial Situation:

Begin by evaluating your current income, expenses, and any existing savings. Determine your monthly living expenses, including housing, utilities, groceries, transportation, and debt payments. This baseline will help you set a realistic savings goal.

Example: Suppose your monthly expenses total $3,000. Aim to save at least three to six months' worth, or $9,000 to $18,000, for a robust emergency fund.

2. Set Clear Objectives:

Define specific goals for your emergency fund based on your financial obligations and risk tolerance. Consider factors such as job stability, health status, and potential emergencies unique to your circumstances.

Example: If you work in a volatile industry or have dependents, aim for a larger emergency fund to cover prolonged periods of financial uncertainty.

3. Start Small, but Start Now:

Even if you can only afford to save a small amount each month, consistency is key. Automate contributions to your emergency fund to ensure regular savings without temptation to spend.

Example: Commit to setting aside $100 or 5% of your monthly income, whichever is feasible, into a separate savings account dedicated to emergencies.

4. Prioritize High-Yield Savings:

Maximize the growth potential of your emergency fund by choosing a high-yield savings account or a money market account with competitive interest rates. While traditional savings accounts offer stability, explore options that optimize returns while maintaining accessibility.

Example: Research online banks or credit unions offering APY (Annual Percentage Yield) rates higher than the national average to maximize your savings over time.

5. Adjust and Reassess:

As your financial situation evolves, periodically review and adjust your emergency fund goals and contributions. Windfalls such as tax refunds or bonuses can bolster your fund, while unexpected expenses may necessitate temporary adjustments to your savings plan.

Example: Reassess your emergency fund target annually or after major life events such as marriage, childbirth, or career changes to ensure alignment with your current needs.

Sumarily, building an emergency fund in 2024 requires proactive planning, disciplined saving habits, and flexibility to adapt to changing circumstances. By following these steps and tailoring them to your individual situation, you can cultivate financial resilience and navigate unforeseen challenges with confidence.

Start today, and empower yourself to face whatever the future may hold.

INTRODUCTION TO INVESTMENT VEHICLES

Investing is a cornerstone of financial growth and security, but for many, the world of investment vehicles can seem daunting and complex. Understanding the basics of investment vehicles is crucial for anyone looking to build wealth over time. Let's provide you a practical introduction to investment vehicles, outlining their types, characteristics, and steps to create a realistic investment strategy.

Types of Investment Vehicles:

1. Stocks: Stocks represent ownership in a company and offer the potential for capital appreciation and dividends.

2. Bonds: Bonds are debt securities issued by governments or corporations, providing fixed interest payments over time.

3. Mutual Funds: Mutual funds pool money from multiple investors to invest in a diversified portfolio of stocks, bonds, or other assets.

4. Exchange-Traded Funds (ETFs): ETFs are similar to mutual funds but trade on stock exchanges like individual stocks, offering intraday trading flexibility.

5. Real Estate Investment Trusts (REITs): REITs allow investors to own and benefit from income-generating real estate properties without direct ownership responsibilities.

6. Commodities: Commodities include physical goods like gold, oil, or agricultural products, offering diversification and hedging against inflation.

STEPS TO CREATE A REALISTIC INVESTMENT STRATEGY:

1. Define Your Goals: Determine your investment objectives, whether it's wealth accumulation, retirement planning, or saving for a specific milestone.

2. Assess Risk Tolerance: Understand your risk tolerance by considering factors such as investment timeline, financial obligations, and comfort with market fluctuations.

3. Diversification: Spread your investments across different asset classes and investment vehicles to reduce risk and optimize returns.

4. Research and Due Diligence: Conduct thorough research on potential investments, considering factors like historical performance, fees, and management expertise.

5. Asset Allocation: Allocate your investment capital among different asset classes based on your risk tolerance and investment goals.

6. Monitor and Adjust: Regularly review your investment portfolio, monitor performance, and make adjustments as needed to stay aligned with your objectives.

Example Scenario:

Suppose Anna, a 35-year-old investor, aims to build wealth for retirement over the next 25 years. After assessing her risk tolerance and financial situation, she decides on a diversified investment strategy:

- 60% allocation to stocks for long-term growth potential.

- 30% allocation to bonds for income generation and risk mitigation.

- 10% allocation to real estate investment trusts (REITs) for added diversification and passive income.

Anna periodically reviews her portfolio, rebalancing as necessary to maintain her target asset allocation and stay on track towards her retirement goals.

Understanding investment vehicles and creating a realistic investment strategy are essential steps towards financial success. By following these principles and tailoring them to individual circumstances, investors can build portfolios that align with their goals and risk tolerance, ultimately achieving long-term financial security.

DIVERSIFICATION AND RISK MANAGEMENT

Diversification and risk management are fundamental principles in the realm of investment strategy. They serve as pillars for building resilient portfolios capable of withstanding market turbulence while aiming for long-term growth. Understanding these concepts and implementing them effectively is crucial for investors seeking to optimize returns while mitigating potential losses. Here, we'll delve into practical steps for creating a realistic diversification and risk management plan, along with illustrative examples.

1. Assessing Risk Tolerance: Begin by evaluating your risk tolerance. Understand your financial goals, investment timeline, and willingness to endure fluctuations in the value of your portfolio.

2. Asset Allocation: Diversify across asset classes such as stocks, bonds, real estate, and commodities. Allocate your investments based on your risk tolerance and investment horizon. For instance, younger investors with a higher risk tolerance may lean towards a more equity-heavy allocation, while those nearing retirement may opt for a more conservative mix.

3. Diversification within Asset Classes: Within each asset class, spread investments across different sectors or industries. For example, instead of investing solely in technology stocks, consider diversifying across healthcare, consumer goods, and financial sectors. This minimizes exposure to sector-specific risks.

4. Geographical Diversification: Invest in various regions or countries to reduce the impact of geopolitical events, economic downturns, or currency fluctuations. For instance, an investor in the United States may diversify by including international stocks or emerging market funds in their portfolio.

5. Risk-Adjusted Returns: Evaluate investments not only based on potential returns but also on risk-adjusted returns. Some investments may offer high returns but come with significant volatility. Analyze the risk-return tradeoff to ensure it aligns with your risk appetite.

6. Periodic Review and Rebalancing: Regularly review your portfolio's performance and rebalance if necessary. Market fluctuations may cause your asset allocation to deviate from the original plan. Rebalancing involves selling overperforming assets and buying underperforming ones to maintain the desired allocation.

7. Utilize Risk Management Tools: Consider employing risk management tools such as stop-loss orders, options, or hedging strategies to protect your portfolio from downside risks. These tools can help limit losses during market downturns while allowing for participation in potential upside movements.

8. Stay Informed and Seek Professional Advice: Stay updated on market trends, economic indicators, and geopolitical events that may impact your investments. Consider consulting with financial advisors or investment professionals to gain insights and expertise in crafting a robust diversification and risk management strategy.

Effective diversification and risk management are essential components of a successful investment strategy. Remember, diversification does not guarantee profits or protect against losses, but it can help mitigate risks and enhance overall portfolio stability.

CHAPTER FOUR

DEBT MANAGEMENT

Are you tired of feeling overwhelmed by debt? Do you find yourself trapped in a cycle of borrowing, struggling to make ends meet? Take a deep breath, because there's hope. Debt management doesn't have to be a mystery reserved for financial wizards. With the right knowledge and strategies, anyone can take control of their finances and pave the way to a brighter, debt-free future.

UNDERSTANDING DEBT

Let's start with the basics. Debt is simply money that you owe to someone else. Whether it's a credit card balance, a student loan, or a mortgage, borrowing money comes with the responsibility to repay it, usually with added interest. While debt can be a useful tool for achieving goals like buying a home or investing in education, it can also become burdensome if not managed properly.

THE PROBLEM WITH DEBT

Debt becomes problematic when it spirals out of control, leading to financial stress and limiting your ability to build wealth and pursue your dreams. High-interest rates, late fees, and penalties can quickly escalate what you owe, making it even harder to dig yourself out of the hole. Moreover, excessive debt can damage your credit score, making it harder to secure loans or even rent an apartment in the future.

STEPS TO EFFECTIVE DEBT MANAGEMENT

1. Face the Numbers: The first step in managing debt is to understand exactly how much you owe and to whom. Take stock of all your debts, including balances, interest rates, and minimum payments.

2. Create a Budget: A budget is your roadmap to financial stability. Track your income and expenses to identify areas where you can cut back and allocate more money toward debt repayment.

3. Prioritize Repayment: Not all debts are created equal. Start by tackling high-interest debts first, as they cost you the most in the long run. Make minimum payments on all debts while directing any extra funds towards the one with the highest interest rate.

4. Explore Consolidation: Consolidating multiple debts into a single loan with a lower interest rate can simplify repayment and reduce overall costs. However, be cautious and ensure that you're not trading short-term relief for long-term financial strain.

5. Negotiate with Creditors: Don't hesitate to reach out to your creditors if you're struggling to make payments. Many lenders are willing to negotiate lower interest rates or more manageable payment plans, especially if it means they'll get their money back.

6. Seek Professional Help if Needed: If your debt feels insurmountable or if you're unsure where to start, consider seeking help from a certified credit counselor or financial advisor. They can provide personalized guidance and resources to help you get back on track.

THE ROAD TO FINANCIAL FREEDOM

Managing debt isn't just about making minimum payments and crossing your fingers. It's about taking control of your financial future and empowering yourself to live a life free from the shackles of debt. By facing your finances head-on, creating a plan, and sticking to it, you can break free from the cycle of borrowing and build a more secure and prosperous tomorrow. Remember, the journey may not be easy, but the destination—financial freedom—is well worth the effort.

STRATEGIES FOR PAYING OFF DEBT

Debt can feel like a heavy burden, but it doesn't have to weigh you down forever. With the right strategies, you can take control of your finances and work towards a debt-free future. We'll explore some simple yet powerful techniques that anyone can use to pay off debt and achieve financial freedom.

1. Assess Your Debt: The first step in tackling debt is to understand exactly what you owe. Make a list of all your debts, including the amount owed, interest rates, and minimum monthly payments. This clear picture will help you prioritize which debts to focus on first.

2. Create a Budget: A budget is a roadmap for your finances, showing you where your money is going each month. Start by tracking your income and expenses to see where you can cut back. Allocate as much money as possible towards paying off debt while still covering essential expenses.

3. Prioritize High-Interest Debts: High-interest debts, like credit card balances, can quickly spiral out of control if left unchecked. Focus on paying off these debts first, as they are costing you the most money in interest charges. Consider transferring balances to lower-interest cards or consolidating debts with a personal loan.

4. Use the Debt Snowball or Avalanche Method: Two popular debt repayment strategies are the snowball and avalanche methods. With the snowball method, you pay off your smallest debts first, gaining momentum as you see quick wins. The avalanche method prioritizes debts with the highest interest rates, saving you money in the long run.

5. Increase Your Income: Increasing your income can accelerate your debt payoff journey. Look for ways to earn extra money, whether through a side hustle, freelance work, or asking for a raise at your current job.

Every additional dollar you earn can be put towards paying off debt faster.

6. Cut Expenses: Take a close look at your spending habits and identify areas where you can cut back. Cancel unnecessary subscriptions, dine out less often, and find creative ways to save on everyday expenses. Redirect the money you save towards your debt repayment goals.

7. Celebrate Milestones: Paying off debt is a significant accomplishment, so don't forget to celebrate your progress along the way. Set milestones for yourself, such as paying off a certain percentage of your debt or reaching a specific dollar amount. Reward yourself for hitting these milestones to stay motivated.

8. Seek Support: Managing debt can be challenging, but you don't have to do it alone. Seek support from friends, family, or a financial advisor who can offer guidance and encouragement. Joining online communities or support groups can also connect you with others who are on a similar journey.

Paying off debt requires patience, discipline, and determination, but it is entirely achievable with the right strategies in place. Remember to celebrate your progress along the way and seek support when needed. With dedication and perseverance, you can master your debt and pave the way to financial freedom.

LEVERAGING DEBT WISELY

Are you curious about how to make debt work for you rather than against you? It's a common misconception that all debt is bad, but the truth is, when used wisely, debt can be a powerful tool for building wealth and achieving your financial goals. Let's embark on a journey to understand how to leverage debt intelligently and responsibly.

Understanding Debt: Debt is simply money borrowed with the promise to repay it later, usually with interest. There are two primary types of debt: good debt and bad debt.

Good Debt vs. Bad Debt: Good debt typically refers to loans or investments that have the potential to increase in value over time or generate income. Examples include mortgages for real estate, student loans for education, or business loans for entrepreneurship. On the other hand, bad debt typically refers to high-interest consumer debt used to purchase depreciating assets or non-essential items, such as credit card debt for luxury goods or high-interest personal loans.

The Power of Leverage: Leveraging debt involves using borrowed funds to amplify potential returns or achieve financial objectives that would be difficult to accomplish with cash alone. For instance, taking out a mortgage allows you to own a home and potentially benefit from its appreciation over time, while only putting down a fraction of the purchase price as a down payment.

STRATEGIC DEBT MANAGEMENT

To leverage debt wisely, it's crucial to have a strategic plan in place. This involves:

Budgeting and Planning: Understanding your financial situation, setting clear goals, and creating a budget that accounts for debt repayment and future investments.

Interest Rates and Terms: Comparing interest rates and terms from various lenders to secure the most favorable borrowing conditions.

Risk Assessment: Evaluating the risks associated with taking on debt, including the potential for fluctuating interest rates or changes in income.

Diversification: Spreading out debt across different assets or investments to mitigate risk and maximize potential returns.

Emergency Fund: Maintaining an emergency fund to cover unexpected expenses and avoid relying solely on credit in times of financial strain.

Building Wealth Over Time: When used strategically, debt can be a stepping stone to wealth accumulation. By investing in assets that appreciate in value or generate income, such as real estate, stocks, or businesses, you can potentially earn returns that exceed the cost of borrowing, thereby increasing your net worth over time.

Risks and Considerations: While leveraging debt can offer significant benefits, it's essential to proceed with caution and be mindful of the risks involved. High levels of debt can increase financial stress and limit flexibility, especially if interest rates rise or income decreases unexpectedly. Additionally, taking on too much debt without a clear plan for repayment can lead to financial hardship and negatively impact credit scores.

Seeking Professional Guidance: If you're unsure about how to leverage debt effectively or navigate complex financial decisions, consider seeking advice from a qualified financial advisor. A professional can help assess your individual circumstances, develop a personalized strategy, and provide ongoing support to help you achieve your financial goals.

Leveraging debt wisely can be a powerful tool for building wealth and achieving financial independence. By understanding the difference between good debt and bad debt, strategically managing your borrowing, and investing in assets that have the potential to grow over time, you can take control of your financial future and create lasting prosperity. Remember, the key is to approach debt with careful consideration, discipline, and a long-term perspective.

CHAPTER FIVE

INCOME GENERATION

In today's rapidly evolving economic landscape, the ability to generate income stands as a cornerstone skill for individuals striving to thrive and prosper. As we traverse the complexities of the year 2024 and beyond, the significance of income generation transcends mere financial stability; it encapsulates adaptability, resilience, and empowerment. Now we will delve into the reasons why income generation has become an indispensable skill for everyone in 2024 looking forward.

First and foremost, the traditional career trajectory has undergone a profound metamorphosis in recent years. The days of lifelong employment with a single company are increasingly becoming obsolete, replaced by a gig economy characterized by freelancing, remote work, and project-based engagements. In this fluid job market, individuals who possess the prowess to create income streams independent of conventional employment find themselves better equipped to navigate the uncertainties of employment disruptions and economic downturns. Thus, income generation not only provides financial sustenance but also fosters a sense of security amidst the flux of modern employment dynamics.

Moreover, the democratization of technology has democratized entrepreneurship, offering unprecedented opportunities for individuals to monetize their skills and passions. The advent of social media, e-commerce platforms, and digital marketing channels has dismantled traditional barriers to entry, enabling aspiring entrepreneurs to reach global audiences with minimal capital investment. Whether it be through launching an online store, monetizing a YouTube channel, or offering freelance services on digital marketplaces, the avenues for income generation are manifold and accessible to anyone with an internet connection and ingenuity. In essence, the ability to harness technology for income generation empowers individuals to transcend geographical constraints and traditional employment paradigms, thereby unlocking boundless opportunities for financial growth and self-realization.

Furthermore, the economic shocks wrought by global crises, such as the COVID-19 pandemic, have underscored the fragility of relying solely on a single source of income. As millions found themselves grappling with unemployment and financial insecurity, the importance of diversifying income streams became glaringly evident. Those who had cultivated supplementary sources of income, whether through investments, side hustles, or passive income streams, were better equipped to weather the storm and mitigate the adverse effects of economic upheaval. Thus, in an era characterized by volatility and uncertainty, the ability to diversify income streams serves as a bulwark against financial instability, empowering individuals to safeguard their livelihoods and futures.

Moreover, income generation fosters a culture of self-reliance and entrepreneurial mindset, which are indispensable traits in an increasingly competitive and innovation-driven global economy. By cultivating a proactive approach to wealth creation and seizing opportunities for value creation, individuals not only enhance their earning potential but also cultivate a mindset of abundance and possibility. This entrepreneurial mindset extends beyond mere financial gain; it encompasses resilience in the face of setbacks, creativity in problem-solving, and a relentless pursuit of personal and professional growth. In essence, income generation transcends the realm of finances; it fosters a mindset of empowerment and agency, equipping individuals with the tools to chart their own destinies and shape their desired futures.

So, the year 2024 heralds a paradigm shift in the way we perceive income generation. No longer relegated to the realm of entrepreneurs and business tycoons, the ability to generate income has emerged as a fundamental skillset for everyone seeking to thrive in the modern economy. Whether through leveraging technology, diversifying income streams, or cultivating an entrepreneurial mindset, income generation empowers individuals to transcend the limitations of traditional employment and seize control of their financial destinies. As we navigate the complexities of the 21st century, the imperative of income generation stands as a beacon of opportunity, guiding individuals towards prosperity, resilience, and self-actualization.

MAXIMIZING YOUR EARNING POTENTIAL

Maximizing your earning potential requires strategic planning and proactive efforts. Whether you're aiming for a higher salary in your current role or exploring new career opportunities, implementing a well-defined plan can significantly enhance your financial prospects. Here are practical steps to help you create a realistic strategy for maximizing your earning potential:

1. Self-Assessment:

Begin by evaluating your skills, experiences, and qualifications. Identify your strengths, areas for improvement, and the value you bring to employers. Consider factors such as education, certifications, specialized skills, and relevant experience. Conducting a thorough self-assessment will provide clarity on where you stand and what steps you need to take to progress.

Example: Joy, a marketing professional, assessed her expertise in digital marketing and identified areas for skill enhancement such as data analytics and social media advertising.

2. Set Clear Goals:

Define specific and measurable financial goals that align with your career aspirations. Determine your target income level and the timeframe for achieving it. Break down your goals into achievable milestones to track your progress effectively.

Example: John aims to increase his annual income by 20% within the next two years through salary increments and freelance projects.

3. Invest in Continuous Learning:

Stay updated with industry trends, technologies, and best practices by investing in ongoing learning and development. Acquire new skills, pursue relevant certifications, attend workshops, and participate in networking events to expand your knowledge base and enhance your marketability.

Example: Emily enrolled in an online course on project management to complement her existing skill set and increase her chances of securing a higher-paying role.

4. Leverage Negotiation Skills:

Develop strong negotiation skills to advocate for yourself during salary discussions and job offers. Research industry salary benchmarks, demonstrate your value proposition to employers, and confidently negotiate for competitive compensation packages.

Example: Mike successfully negotiated a higher salary and additional benefits by showcasing his track record of achieving measurable results during the interview process.

5. Explore Diverse Income Streams:

Diversify your income sources to maximize your earning potential. Consider freelance work, consulting gigs, passive income streams, or investment opportunities that complement your expertise and interests.

Example: David, a software developer, earns additional income by freelancing on platforms like Upwork and investing in dividend-paying stocks.

By following these practical steps and tailoring them to your unique circumstances, you can create a realistic plan to maximize your earning potential. Remember to stay proactive, adaptable, and focused on continuous improvement to achieve your financial goals and advance your career successfully.

EXPLORING PASSIVE INCOME STREAMS

In the scope of personal finance, the pursuit of passive income has become a beacon for those seeking financial independence and freedom from traditional employment constraints. Passive income, often dubbed as the holy grail of wealth-building, offers the allure of earning money with minimal ongoing effort. While achieving complete passivity may be elusive, exploring various passive income streams can significantly augment your earnings and provide financial stability. Let's delve into practical steps to explore and leverage passive income streams, supplemented with realistic examples and accessible platforms.

Understanding Passive Income

Passive income refers to earnings derived from ventures in which the individual's involvement is minimal after the initial setup. Contrary to active income, which requires ongoing time and effort (like a salaried job), passive income continues to flow even when you're not actively working. Embracing passive income involves diversifying revenue streams through investments, digital assets, or creative endeavors.

Practical Steps to Explore Passive Income

1. Identify Your Skills and Assets

Assess your skills, expertise, and assets that can be monetized passively.

Examples: Photography skills for stock photo sales, coding abilities for app development, or owning rental property for passive rental income.

2. Research Passive Income Opportunities

Explore various passive income opportunities, including:

Dividend Investing: Platforms like Robinhood, M1 Finance, or Vanguard offer dividend-paying stocks or ETFs.

Peer-to-Peer Lending: Websites like Prosper or LendingClub facilitate peer-to-peer lending, earning interest on loans.

Digital Products: Create and sell digital products such as e-books, online courses, or stock photos through platforms like Gumroad, Teachable, or Shutterstock.

Rental Income: Utilize platforms like Airbnb or Vrbo for short-term rental income, or hire a property management company for long-term rentals.

Affiliate Marketing: Join affiliate programs through websites like Amazon Associates, ShareASale, or ClickBank to earn commissions by promoting products.

3. Start Small and Scale

Begin with low-risk ventures and gradually scale up as you gain confidence and experience.

Diversify your passive income streams to minimize risk and maximize potential earnings.

4. Automate and Delegate

Leverage automation tools and outsourcing services to streamline processes and reduce active involvement.

Use apps like Zapier for workflow automation or hire virtual assistants through platforms like Upwork or Fiverr for tasks requiring human intervention.

5. Monitor and Optimize

Continuously monitor the performance of your passive income streams and optimize strategies for better results.

Stay informed about market trends and adjust your portfolio or offerings accordingly.

Realistic Examples and Platforms

Dividend Investing: Start investing in dividend-paying stocks through platforms like Robinhood or Vanguard.

Digital Products: Create an online course on a topic you're knowledgeable about and sell it on platforms like Teachable or Udemy.

Rental Income: Rent out a spare room on Airbnb or Vrbo to earn extra income from your property.

Affiliate Marketing: Join the Amazon Associates program and promote products relevant to your audience through your blog or social media.

Exploring passive income streams offers a pathway to financial security and independence. By identifying viable opportunities, starting small, and leveraging available platforms and tools, anyone can embark on the journey towards building a diversified portfolio of passive income streams. Remember, consistency, patience, and adaptability are key to success in this endeavor. Start today and pave the way for a more financially abundant future.

CHAPTER SIX

REAL ESTATE INVESTING

In 2024, the allure of real estate has transcended its traditional appeal, emerging as a must-have skill for individuals across diverse demographics. This surge in popularity can be attributed to several factors, each intertwined with the evolving landscape of global economies, societal shifts, and technological advancements.

First and foremost, the enduring stability and potential for wealth accumulation inherent in real estate investment have solidified its status as a coveted asset class. Amid economic uncertainties and volatile financial markets, tangible assets like properties offer a sense of security and long-term value appreciation. As traditional investment avenues face disruptions and fluctuating returns, real estate stands out as a reliable source of passive income and capital preservation.

Moreover, the democratization of real estate investment facilitated by innovative platforms and technologies has broadened its accessibility. Crowdfunding platforms, fractional ownership models, and digital marketplaces have empowered individuals with limited capital to participate in lucrative real estate ventures previously reserved for institutional investors. This democratization not only fosters financial inclusivity but also cultivates a culture of entrepreneurship and wealth creation among aspiring investors.

In parallel, the paradigm shift towards remote work and decentralized living arrangements has catalyzed a reevaluation of housing preferences and lifestyle choices.

The COVID-19 pandemic accelerated trends towards suburban migration, remote-friendly locales, and flexible living arrangements, prompting individuals to prioritize real estate investments aligned with their evolving needs and preferences. As remote work becomes entrenched in mainstream culture, the demand for residential properties offering space, privacy, and connectivity continues to surge, driving investment opportunities in burgeoning markets.

Furthermore, the emergence of sustainability and environmental consciousness as paramount considerations in decision-making processes has reshaped the real estate landscape. Eco-friendly developments, energy-efficient designs, and sustainable practices not only align with ethical imperatives but also resonate with discerning consumers and investors seeking socially responsible investment opportunities. As sustainability becomes synonymous with value creation and future-proofing, real estate professionals equipped with the knowledge and expertise to navigate eco-conscious markets gain a competitive edge in an increasingly discerning marketplace.

The burgeoning popularity of real estate as a must-have skill in 2024 is emblematic of its enduring appeal and transformative potential in an era defined by economic uncertainty, technological disruption, and shifting societal norms. As individuals recognize the intrinsic value of real estate as a wealth-building tool, a means of financial empowerment, and a reflection of evolving lifestyle preferences, cultivating proficiency in real estate investment and management emerges as a strategic imperative for success in an ever-evolving world.

Whether as investors, homeowners, or professionals within the industry, mastery of real estate fundamentals empowers individuals to navigate complex market dynamics, capitalize on emerging opportunities, and chart a course towards financial prosperity and personal fulfillment in the years to come.

UNDERSTANDING REAL ESTATE AS AN INVESTMENT

Real estate investment presents a compelling opportunity for wealth creation and portfolio diversification. However, navigating the complexities of the real estate market requires understanding its fundamentals and employing strategic approaches. Take a look at the essential steps to comprehend real estate as an investment, offering realistic examples and recommending tools and platforms to facilitate the process.

Step 1: Educate Yourself

Before diving into real estate investment, it's crucial to educate yourself about the market dynamics, investment strategies, and potential risks. Resources such as books, online courses, and reputable websites like Investopedia, BiggerPockets, and NerdWallet offer comprehensive information on real estate investment fundamentals.

Step 2: Define Your Investment Goals and Strategy

Clarify your investment objectives, whether it's generating rental income, long-term appreciation, or a combination of both. Develop a coherent investment strategy based on your financial goals, risk tolerance, and time horizon. For instance, if you seek steady cash flow, consider investing in rental properties, whereas if you aim for capital appreciation, explore options like house flipping or commercial real estate.

Step 3: Assess Your Financial Position

Evaluate your financial situation, including your credit score, savings, and debt-to-income ratio. Determine how much capital you can allocate to real estate investment without jeopardizing your financial stability. Additionally, consider factors like closing costs, property taxes, maintenance expenses, and potential vacancies when calculating your investment budget.

Step 4: Research and Analyze Properties

Conduct thorough research on properties in your target market. Analyze factors such as location, property type, market trends, rental demand, and potential appreciation. Utilize online platforms like Zillow, Realtor.com, and Redfin to browse listings, compare prices, and assess property values. Employ real estate investment analysis tools like Mashvisor or DealCheck to evaluate the financial viability of prospective properties, including cash flow projections, cap rates, and return on investment (ROI).

Step 5: Financing Your Investment

Explore financing options tailored to your investment strategy and financial profile. Traditional avenues like mortgages, FHA loans, or conventional bank loans are viable for long-term investments. Alternatively, consider alternative financing options such as hard money loans or crowdfunding platforms like RealtyMogul or Fundrise for shorter-term or high-return projects.

Step 6: Execute Due Diligence

Before finalizing a purchase, conduct due diligence to mitigate risks and ensure a sound investment decision. This includes property inspections, reviewing legal documents (e.g., title deeds, lease agreements), and assessing potential liabilities or encumbrances. Engage professionals like real estate agents, inspectors, and attorneys to facilitate the due diligence process and provide expert guidance.

Step 7: Manage Your Investment

Once you've acquired a property, effective management is essential to maximize returns and mitigate risks. Implement sound property management practices, such as regular maintenance, tenant screening, rent collection, and proactive communication. Leverage property management software like Buildium, AppFolio, or Cozy to streamline administrative tasks, track expenses, and communicate with tenants efficiently.

Real estate investment can be a lucrative endeavor with the right knowledge, strategy, and execution. By following these practical steps and leveraging available resources and technologies, you can navigate the complexities of the real estate market and build a successful investment portfolio. Remember to continuously educate yourself, adapt to market dynamics, and seek professional advice when needed to optimize your investment journey.

TIPS FOR SUCCESSFUL REAL ESTATE VENTURES

Real estate ventures offer lucrative opportunities for investors to build wealth, generate passive income, and diversify their portfolios. However, navigating the complexities of the real estate market requires a strategic approach and careful planning. In this guide, we will explore practical tips for success in real estate ventures, accompanied by actionable steps and realistic examples.

1. Conduct Thorough Market Research:

Before diving into any real estate venture, it's crucial to conduct thorough market research to understand current trends, property values, rental rates, and demand-supply dynamics in your target area. Utilize online platforms such as Zillow, Realtor.com, or Redfin to gather data on property prices, rental yields, and market trends. Additionally, leverage tools like Mashvisor or NeighborhoodScout for comprehensive neighborhood analysis and insights.

2. Set Clear Investment Goals:

Define your investment goals and objectives to guide your real estate ventures effectively. Whether your aim is to generate rental income, flip properties for quick profits, or build long-term wealth through appreciation, setting clear goals will help you make informed decisions and stay focused on your investment strategy.

3. Create a Detailed Financial Plan:

Develop a comprehensive financial plan that outlines your budget, financing options, and projected returns. Consider factors such as down payment, closing costs, renovation expenses, property taxes, insurance, and ongoing maintenance costs. Utilize financial planning tools like Personal Capital or Mint to track expenses, manage cash flow, and monitor investment performance.

4. Build a Reliable Network:

Networking is essential in the real estate industry. Connect with real estate agents, brokers, lenders, contractors, property managers, and fellow investors to expand your network and access valuable resources and opportunities. Platforms like BiggerPockets offer a vibrant online community of real estate professionals where you can learn, collaborate, and network with like-minded individuals.

5. Conduct Due Diligence:

Perform thorough due diligence on properties before making any investment decisions. Inspect the property for structural issues, conduct a title search, review zoning regulations, and assess potential risks and liabilities. Utilize inspection services like HomeAdvisor or Angie's List to find reputable inspectors and contractors for property evaluations.

6. Implement a Strategic Marketing Plan:

If you're involved in property flipping or rental investments, implementing a strategic marketing plan is essential to attract buyers or tenants. Utilize online listing platforms such as Zillow, Trulia, or Craigslist to showcase your properties to a wide audience. Additionally, leverage social media channels, email marketing, and professional photography to enhance your property's visibility and appeal.

7. Stay Informed and Adapt:

The real estate market is dynamic and subject to constant changes. Stay informed about industry trends, regulatory developments, and economic indicators that may impact your investments. Subscribe to industry publications, attend networking events, and seek professional advice to stay ahead of the curve and adapt your strategy accordingly.

Successful real estate ventures require a combination of strategic planning, market knowledge, financial acumen, and effective execution. By following these practical tips and steps, investors can navigate the complexities of the real estate market with confidence and achieve their investment goals. Additionally, leveraging technology and online resources such as real estate platforms, financial tools, and networking platforms can streamline the investment process and enhance overall efficiency and success.

Remember, patience, persistence, and continuous learning are key to long-term success in real estate ventures. By staying disciplined, adaptable, and informed, investors can unlock the full potential of real estate as a wealth-building asset class.

CHAPTER SEVEN

RETIREMENT PLANNING

Retirement planning is not merely a matter of fiscal responsibility; it's a fundamental aspect of securing one's future and maintaining financial independence. In today's dynamic economic landscape, characterized by longer life expectancies and evolving retirement structures, effective retirement planning has become more crucial than ever. This chapter elucidates why everyone, irrespective of age, should take retirement planning seriously. It further outlines the essence of retirement planning and provides pragmatic strategies for individuals of all ages to plan effectively for their retirement in 2024.

The Imperative of Retirement Planning:

Retirement planning is not a luxury; it's a necessity. It ensures financial stability during the post-employment phase, allowing individuals to maintain their desired standard of living and pursue their aspirations without being burdened by financial constraints. Failing to plan for retirement can lead to a precarious situation, where individuals may face difficulties in covering basic expenses, accessing healthcare, or enjoying a comfortable lifestyle.

Moreover, the traditional notion of retirement has evolved significantly. With advancements in healthcare and improvements in lifestyle, people are living longer, necessitating more substantial retirement savings to sustain themselves over an extended period. Additionally, the shift from defined benefit pension plans to defined contribution plans places greater responsibility on individuals to manage their retirement funds effectively. Hence, the need for proactive retirement planning is paramount to navigate these changes successfully.

Understanding Retirement Planning:

At its core, retirement planning entails assessing one's financial goals, estimating future expenses, and devising strategies to accumulate sufficient funds to meet those needs during retirement. It involves a comprehensive analysis of income sources, including savings, investments, pensions, and social security benefits, juxtaposed against anticipated expenses such as housing, healthcare, leisure activities, and unforeseen contingencies.

Effective retirement planning encompasses various elements, including:

Setting Clear Goals: Establishing specific retirement goals based on individual aspirations, lifestyle preferences, and anticipated expenses is foundational to the planning process. Whether it's traveling the world, pursuing hobbies, or maintaining a modest lifestyle, defining these objectives provides a roadmap for financial planning.

Budgeting and Saving: Developing a disciplined approach towards budgeting and saving is indispensable for building a robust retirement corpus. Setting aside a portion of income for retirement savings, leveraging tax-advantaged retirement accounts like 401(k)s, IRAs, or pension schemes, and automating contributions facilitate consistent wealth accumulation over time.

Diversified Investments: Adopting a diversified investment strategy is vital for mitigating risks and optimizing returns. Allocating assets across a mix of equities, bonds, real estate, and other investment vehicles tailored to individual risk tolerance and time horizon enhances portfolio resilience and growth potential.

Monitoring and Adjusting: Regularly monitoring the progress of retirement savings and adjusting investment strategies in response to changing market conditions, life events, or financial goals ensures alignment with long-term objectives. Rebalancing portfolios, optimizing asset allocation, and maximizing employer-sponsored retirement benefits contribute to sustaining financial viability in retirement.

Pragmatic Strategies for Effective Retirement Planning in 2024:

Regardless of age, adopting a proactive approach towards retirement planning is imperative for securing financial well-being in the future. Here are pragmatic strategies tailored to different life stages:

Young Adults (20s-30s):

Start Early: Take advantage of the power of compounding by initiating retirement savings as soon as possible.

Maximize Contributions: Contribute the maximum allowable amount to employer-sponsored retirement plans and explore additional retirement account options.

Invest Aggressively: Embrace a growth-oriented investment strategy with a higher allocation towards equities to capitalize on long-term wealth accumulation.

Mid-Career Professionals (40s-50s):

Assess Progress: Evaluate retirement savings goals vis-a-vis current savings and adjust contributions accordingly.

Prioritize Debt Reduction: Focus on paying off high-interest debts to free up resources for retirement savings.

Consider Catch-Up Contributions: Leverage catch-up contributions allowed for individuals aged 50 and above to accelerate retirement savings.

Pre-Retirees (Late 50s-60s):

Fine-Tune Asset Allocation: Transition towards a more conservative investment approach to safeguard accumulated wealth.

Evaluate Retirement Readiness: Assess retirement income adequacy and explore strategies to bridge potential shortfalls, such as delaying retirement or part-time employment.

Optimize Social Security: Strategize Social Security claiming strategies to maximize benefits over the long term.

Retirement planning is a vital undertaking that demands attention and diligence from individuals across all age groups. By recognizing the imperative of retirement planning, understanding its essence, and implementing pragmatic strategies tailored to their life stages, individuals can fortify their financial futures and embark on retirement with confidence and security. In the dynamic landscape of 2024 and beyond, proactive retirement planning remains the linchpin for achieving financial independence and enjoying a fulfilling post-employment life.

RETIREMENT SAVINGS OPTIONS

Retirement planning is a crucial aspect of financial wellness that requires careful consideration and proactive steps. With the myriad of retirement savings options available, choosing the right strategy can seem daunting. However, by understanding the various avenues and taking actionable steps, individuals can secure their financial future with confidence. Consider the following practical retirement savings options, along with realistic examples and recommended tools to facilitate the process.

Understanding Retirement Savings Options:

1. Employer-Sponsored Retirement Plans:

- ***401(k) Plans****:* Many employers offer 401(k) plans, allowing employees to contribute a portion of their salary pre-tax, often with matching contributions from the employer.

- *403(b) Plans*: Similar to 401(k) plans but offered by certain non-profit organizations, schools, and government entities.

- *Examples*: Fidelity, Vanguard, and Charles Schwab offer platforms for managing employer-sponsored retirement plans.

2. Individual Retirement Accounts (IRAs):

- *Traditional IRAs*: Contributions may be tax-deductible, and earnings grow tax-deferred until withdrawal during retirement.

- *Roth IRAs*: Contributions are made after-tax, but withdrawals in retirement are tax-free.

- *Examples*: Betterment, TD Ameritrade, and E*TRADE provide user-friendly platforms for opening and managing IRA accounts.

3. Health Savings Accounts (HSAs):

- *HSAs offer triple tax advantages*: contributions are tax-deductible, earnings grow tax-free, and withdrawals for qualified medical expenses are tax-free.

- Individuals can use HSA funds for non-medical expenses penalty-free after age 65.

- *Example*: Lively offers an HSA platform with investment options and low fees.

4. Brokerage Accounts:

- Brokerage accounts provide flexibility and accessibility for retirement savings outside of employer-sponsored plans and IRAs.

- Investors can choose from a wide range of investment options, including stocks, bonds, mutual funds, and ETFs.

- *Examples*: Robinhood, M1 Finance, and Webull offer commission-free trading and intuitive platforms for managing brokerage accounts.

Steps to Establish and Grow Retirement Savings:

1. Assess Financial Situation:

- Determine current expenses, income, and existing retirement savings.

- Calculate retirement goals and estimated expenses.

2. Maximize Employer Contributions:

- Contribute enough to employer-sponsored retirement plans to take full advantage of any matching contributions.

3. Open Individual Retirement Accounts:

- Choose between Traditional or Roth IRA based on tax preferences and eligibility.

- Contribute regularly to maximize tax advantages and compound growth.

4. Consider Health Savings Accounts:

- If eligible, contribute to an HSA to cover current medical expenses and save for future healthcare costs in retirement.

5. Diversify Investments:

- Allocate assets across different investment vehicles to manage risk and maximize returns.

- Regularly review and rebalance investment portfolio to align with retirement goals and risk tolerance.

Retirement savings is a journey that requires strategic planning and consistent effort. By leveraging employer-sponsored plans, individual retirement accounts, health savings accounts, and brokerage accounts, individuals can build a robust retirement nest egg. Utilizing user-friendly platforms and apps offered by reputable financial institutions makes it easier to manage and grow retirement savings effectively. Start today and take control of your financial future with confidence.

PLANNING FOR FINANCIAL INDEPENDENCE

Financial independence is a goal many aspire to achieve, where one has enough wealth and resources to sustain their desired lifestyle without relying on employment income. While it may seem daunting, with careful planning and disciplined execution, it's an attainable objective. See the practical steps towards financial independence along with realistic examples and recommended tools to facilitate the journey.

Step 1: Set Clear Goals

Define what financial independence means to you. This could involve determining your desired retirement age, estimating your annual expenses, and setting target savings and investment goals. For example, if you aim to retire at 55 with an annual expense of $50,000, you'll need to save and invest accordingly.

Tools: Personal finance apps like Mint or YNAB can help track expenses and set savings goals.

Step 2: Create a Budget

Develop a comprehensive budget that aligns with your financial goals. Differentiate between essential expenses, discretionary spending, and savings contributions. Monitor and adjust your budget regularly to stay on track.

Example: Allocate 50% of your income to essentials like housing, utilities, and groceries, 30% to discretionary spending like dining out and entertainment, and 20% to savings and investments.

Tools: Budgeting apps such as PocketGuard or EveryDollar offer features to create and manage budgets effortlessly.

Step 3: Build an Emergency Fund

Establish an emergency fund equivalent to 3-6 months of living expenses. This fund acts as a safety net during unforeseen circumstances such as job loss or medical emergencies, preventing you from dipping into long-term investments.

Example: If your monthly expenses amount to $3,000, aim to accumulate $9,000 - $18,000 in your emergency fund.

Tools: High-yield savings accounts like Ally Bank or Marcus by Goldman Sachs offer competitive interest rates for emergency funds.

Step 4: Eliminate Debt

Prioritize paying off high-interest debt like credit cards and personal loans. Adopt strategies such as the debt snowball or avalanche method to accelerate debt repayment. Once debt-free, redirect those funds towards savings and investments.

Example: If you have a credit card balance of $5,000 with an 18% interest rate, allocate extra funds each month to pay it off aggressively.

Tools: Debt payoff apps like Debt Payoff Planner or Undebt.it can help strategize debt repayment and track progress.

Step 5: Invest Wisely

Maximize contributions to retirement accounts like 401(k)s or IRAs, taking advantage of employer matching programs if available. Diversify investments across asset classes such as stocks, bonds, and real estate to mitigate risk and optimize returns over the long term.

Example: Contribute the maximum allowable amount to your employer-sponsored 401(k) plan, especially if your employer matches contributions.

Tools: Robo-advisors like Betterment or Wealthfront offer automated investment management services with low fees and personalized portfolio allocation.

Achieving financial independence requires discipline, patience, and strategic planning. By following these steps and leveraging available resources, you can pave the way towards a financially secure future. Remember, it's never too early or too late to start planning for financial independence.

CHAPTER EIGHT

WEALTH PRESERVATION AND GROWTH

The pursuit of wealth preservation and growth is a crucial endeavor for individuals seeking financial security and prosperity. Whether you're a seasoned investor or just beginning your journey toward financial independence, implementing practical strategies can make all the difference. Here, we outline actionable steps to safeguard and expand your wealth, supported by realistic examples and recommended apps or websites to facilitate the process.

Establish Clear Financial Goals:

Define your short-term and long-term financial objectives, considering factors such as retirement planning, education funds, and emergency savings. Utilize tools like Mint or YNAB (You Need a Budget) to track expenses, set budgetary targets, and monitor progress toward your goals.

Diversify Investment Portfolio:

Spread your investments across various asset classes to mitigate risks associated with market volatility. For instance, allocate funds to stocks, bonds, real estate, and alternative investments like commodities or cryptocurrency. Robo-advisors such as Betterment or Wealthfront offer automated portfolio management tailored to your risk tolerance and financial goals.

Asset Protection Strategies:

Shield your wealth from potential threats such as lawsuits, creditors, or unforeseen liabilities. Establishing trusts, forming LLCs (Limited Liability Companies), or purchasing adequate insurance coverage can safeguard your assets. LegalZoom provides online resources and services for setting up legal entities, while Policygenius offers a platform to compare insurance policies and secure the best coverage for your needs.

Regular Portfolio Rebalancing:

Periodically review and rebalance your investment portfolio to maintain alignment with your risk tolerance and financial objectives. Sell overperforming assets and reinvest proceeds into underperforming ones to restore equilibrium. Tools like Personal Capital offer portfolio analysis and rebalancing features to optimize asset allocation.

Tax Optimization Strategies:

Minimize tax liabilities through strategic tax planning and utilization of tax-efficient investment vehicles such as retirement accounts (e.g., 401(k), IRA), municipal bonds, or Health Savings Accounts (HSAs). Leveraging tax-loss harvesting techniques and maximizing deductions can further enhance tax efficiency. TurboTax or H&R Block provide user-friendly platforms for tax preparation and optimization.

Continuous Education and Research:

Stay informed about market trends, economic indicators, and regulatory changes to make informed investment decisions. Engage in ongoing education through books, seminars, or online courses to enhance financial literacy and investment acumen. Websites like Investopedia or Morningstar offer comprehensive resources and educational materials for investors of all levels.

Emergency Fund and Liquidity Management:

Maintain a sufficient emergency fund equivalent to at least three to six months of living expenses to weather unforeseen financial setbacks. Optimize liquidity by balancing the accessibility of funds with potential returns, considering high-yield savings accounts or short-term CDs (Certificate of Deposits). Ally Bank or Marcus by Goldman Sachs offer competitive interest rates and user-friendly interfaces for managing savings and liquidity needs.

By implementing these practical strategies and leveraging available tools and resources, individuals can effectively preserve and grow their wealth over time. However, it's essential to tailor these approaches to your specific financial situation, risk tolerance, and objectives. Regular review and adjustment of your financial plan are crucial to adapt to changing circumstances and optimize outcomes in pursuit of long-term financial success.

CONTINUOUSLY IMPROVING YOUR FINANCIAL SITUATION

Mastering personal finance isn't just about balancing your checkbook; it's about actively enhancing your financial well-being. Whether you're looking to build savings, reduce debt, or invest wisely, adopting a mindset of continuous improvement is crucial. By implementing practical strategies and utilizing available resources, you can steadily enhance your financial situation and achieve long-term stability. Here's a step-by-step guide to help you embark on this journey:

1. Set Clear Financial Goals: Start by defining your financial objectives. Do you want to save for a down payment on a house, pay off student loans, or retire early? Establishing specific, measurable goals provides a roadmap for your financial journey.

2. Create a Budget: Develop a realistic budget that outlines your income, expenses, and savings targets. Use budgeting apps like Mint, YNAB (You Need a Budget), or PocketGuard to track your spending, identify areas for improvement, and stay accountable to your financial plan.

3. Reduce Expenses: Identify opportunities to trim unnecessary expenses and redirect those funds towards your financial goals. Consider negotiating bills, cutting subscription services you rarely use, or opting for generic brands instead of name brands.

4. Increase Income: Explore ways to boost your income, such as pursuing a side hustle, asking for a raise at work, or investing in your skills to advance your career prospects. Apps like TaskRabbit, Upwork, or Fiverr can connect you with freelance opportunities to supplement your earnings.

5. Manage Debt Wisely: Develop a strategy to tackle high-interest debt systematically. Consider consolidating debt with a lower interest rate, prioritizing repayment of high-interest loans, and negotiating with creditors to lower interest rates or settle debts. Tools like Credit Karma or Tally can help you manage and optimize your debt repayment plan.

6. Build an Emergency Fund: Start building an emergency fund to cover unexpected expenses and mitigate financial setbacks. Aim to save three to six months' worth of living expenses in a high-yield savings account or a money market fund. Apps like Digit or Qapital can automate your savings by analyzing your spending habits and transferring small amounts into your emergency fund regularly.

7. Invest for the Future: Begin investing for long-term growth and wealth accumulation. Utilize investment platforms like Robinhood, Acorns, or Betterment to start investing in stocks, bonds, or exchange-traded funds (ETFs). Diversify your portfolio to minimize risk and maximize returns over time.

8. Educate Yourself: Continuously expand your financial literacy by reading books, listening to podcasts, or attending workshops on personal finance topics. Resources like Investopedia, The Financial Diet, or podcasts like "The Dave Ramsey Show" offer valuable insights and advice on managing money effectively.

9. Review and Adjust Regularly: Periodically review your financial progress and adjust your strategies as needed. Life circumstances, economic conditions, and personal goals may evolve over time, so staying flexible and adaptive is key to long-term financial success.

10. Seek Professional Guidance: Consider consulting with a certified financial planner or advisor to get personalized guidance tailored to your unique financial situation and goals. They can provide expert insights, help you navigate complex financial decisions, and optimize your financial plan for maximum effectiveness.

By implementing these steps and leveraging available resources, you can take control of your financial future and continuously improve your financial situation. Remember, small actions taken consistently can lead to significant progress over time. Start today and commit to the journey of financial empowerment and prosperity.

CHAPTER NINE

CONCLUSION

In the pursuit of financial well-being and wealth accumulation, adopting simplified yet effective strategies is paramount. Let's recap the key strategies outlined in our comprehensive guide to continuously improving your financial situation:

1. **Set Clear Financial Goals**: Define specific, measurable objectives to guide your financial journey.

2. **Create a Budget**: Develop a realistic budget to track income, expenses, and savings targets using apps like Mint or YNAB.

3. **Reduce Expenses**: Identify and cut unnecessary expenses, redirecting funds toward your financial goals.

4. **Increase Income**: Explore opportunities for additional income through side hustles, career advancement, or freelancing platforms like TaskRabbit or Upwork.

5. **Manage Debt Wisely**: Strategically tackle high-interest debt using tools like Credit Karma or Tally to optimize repayment plans.

6. **Build an Emergency Fund**: Save three to six months' worth of living expenses in a high-yield savings account using apps like Digit or Qapital.

7. **Invest for the Future**: Start investing for long-term growth and wealth accumulation with platforms like Robinhood or Betterment.

8. **Educate Yourself**: Continuously expand financial literacy through books, podcasts, or resources like Investopedia or "The Dave Ramsey Show."

9. **Review and Adjust Regularly**: Periodically assess financial progress and adapt strategies to changing circumstances.

10. **Seek Professional Guidance**: Consider consulting with a certified financial planner for personalized advice and optimization of financial plans.

These simplified strategies provide a roadmap for individuals seeking to enhance their financial well-being and build long-term wealth. By implementing these steps and leveraging available resources, you can take control of your financial future and embark on a journey toward prosperity and financial empowerment. Remember, consistency and commitment are key to achieving lasting success in wealth building.

....

Special note to the reader:

Andrew Mark
Wishes you success on your wealth building journey!

www.ingramcontent.com/pod-product-compliance
Lightning Source LLC
Chambersburg PA
CBHW071050290526
45795CB00004B/1422